What's in this book

T0079989

This book belongs to

_____

兴趣小组
Extra-curricular activity groups

学习内容 Contents

沟通 Communication

说出学科名称
Say the names of subjects

背景介绍：
浩浩和小伙伴们在看学校兴趣小组的海报。

生词 New words

★	放学	school is over
★	一起	together
★	听	to listen
★	美术	art
★	数学	mathematics
★	上课	to attend a class
★	作业	school assignment
★	还有	also
	同学	classmate, schoolmate
	操场	playground
	礼堂	hall, auditorium
	地理	geography
	知道	to know

还有很多同学在礼堂。
There are also many students in the hall.

这里还有美术小组和数学小组。
There is also the mathematics group and the art group.

跨学科学习 Project

调查兴趣喜好并画柱状图
Do a survey on extra-curricular
activities and draw a histogram

文化 Cultures

中西方学校中的活动
School activities in the East
and the West

参考答案：
1 Yes, we have many/only a few..
2 Art, because I like to draw./Mathematics, because I like to work with numbers.
3 He will join the Art group because he is smiling at its poster.

Get ready

1 Does your school have any extra-curricular
activity groups?

2 Which activity group do you want to join?

3 Which activity group do you think Hao Hao will join?

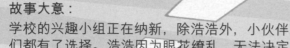
读一读 Read

01

故事大意：
学校的兴趣小组正在纳新，除浩浩外，小伙伴们都有了选择。浩浩因为眼花缭乱，无法决定参加哪个小组。

Extra-curricular
activity groups
→

fàng xué
放学

yī qǐ
一起

放学前，大家一起去报名参加兴趣小组。

参考问题和答案：

1 School is over. How can you tell? (It is half past three in the afternoon.)

2 Where are the children going together? (They are going to see the extra-curricular activity groups.)

4

操场上很热闹，同学们喜欢画画、
唱歌、听音乐。

参考问题和答案：

1 Where is this place? (It is the school playground.)

2 Are there other schoolmates in the playground? (Yes, there are many.)

3 Would you like your school to hold a similar event like this?
(Yes, it looks fun./No.)

美术小组的人最多，同学们的画很
好看。

参考问题和答案：

1 Which activity group has attracted the most schoolmates? (The Art group.)

2 Do you like Art class? Why or why not? (I like it because I like colours a lot./
I don't like it because I am not good at drawing.)

玩数学小组的游戏比上课和做作业
更有趣。

lǐ táng
礼堂

dì lǐ
地理

hái yǒu
还有

"还有"表示在某个范围之外有所补充。
如：这里有同学，还有老师。

还有很多同学在礼堂，因为地理小组的电影很好看。

参考问题和答案：

1　Where is this place? (It is the school hall.)

2　Besides Elsa and Hao Hao, who else is in the hall? (There are many schoolmates there.)

3　Which activity group do you think is showing this film? (The Geography group, because the film is about mountains.)

这里有这么多兴趣小组，浩浩不知道怎么选。

参考问题和答案：

1 What are Hao Hao's friends wearing on their clothes? (They are wearing the badges of the activity groups that they have joined.)

2 Why isn't Hao Hao wearing any badges? (Because he does not know which activity group to join.)

Let's think

1 Recall the story. Match the students to their favourite extra-curricular activity groups. 视情况提醒学生观察第9页人物身上的兴趣小组徽章，进行推断。

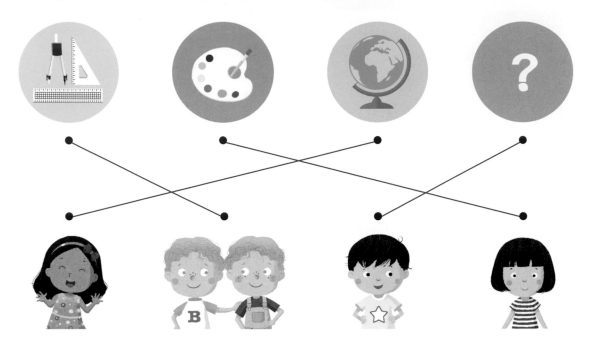

2 Design and draw a badge for your favourite extra-curricular activity group. Tell your friend about it.

向学生介绍在设计兴趣小组的徽章时，应考虑突出兴趣小组的特点，图案以简洁易明为佳。

New words

1 Learn the new words.

上课 / 同学

数学

地理

美术

放学

作业

一起 / 操场

礼堂 / 听

知道 / 还有

2 Listen to your teacher and point to the correct words above.

听听说说 Listen and say

🎧 03 **1** Listen and circle the correct pictures.

1 上课前，玲玲在哪里？

2 放学后，谁和玲玲在一起？

3 玲玲去了哪个小组？

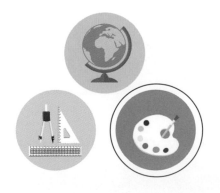

🎧 04 **2** Look at the pictures. Listen to the story a

放学了，你们去哪里？

我去礼堂看地理电影。

我去操场画画，还有几个同学去听音乐。

3 Write the letters and say.

a 作业　　b 数学
c 还有　　d 美术

我喜欢 __d__，因为
我喜欢画画。

我最喜欢 __b__。
__c__ 英语也很有趣。

 我们去做好玩的数学作业。

 我不知道做什么。

 我们一起听音乐吧。

放学后，我们一
起做地理 __a__。

Task

可提高活动难度，如设谈话内容不少于 X 句或不低于 Y 分钟的方式让学生尽量练习中文口语表达和沟通。

Paste a photo of your school and talk about it with your friend.

Paste your photo here.

这是我的学校(school)。
学校的操场和礼堂很大。
我在学校学数学、英语、
美术……我喜欢上课。

Game

Look at the picture and circle the correct words. Then read aloud the paragragh.

他是(男孩/女孩)。
他喜欢(地理/
篮球)，不喜欢
(美术/唱歌)。还有
他的(数学/英语)
很好。

Chant

Listen and say. `05`

学生先将儿歌中出现的兴趣小组全部圈出，再挑选一个自己最喜欢的兴趣小组，牢记于心。全班朗读儿歌时，当读到自己的兴趣小组便举起手。看看选择哪个兴趣小组的人数最多。

操场、教室、礼堂，
你去哪里？
美术、地理、数学，
你学什么？

兴趣小组真有趣，
我最喜欢哪一个，
你知道吗？
你知道吗？

生活用语 Daily expressions

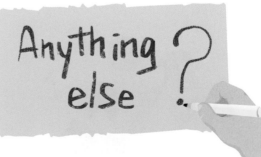

一起去吧。
Let's go together.

还有什么？
Anything else?

写一写 Write

1 Trace and write the characters.

丶 丨 ㇆ 口 吖 吖 听 听

听	听	听	听

丶 丶 ㇀ ㇛ 兴 学 学 学

学	学	学	学

提醒学生"学"的上部是
两点一撇而不是三点。

2 Write and say.

他们喜欢 听 音乐。

这是我的同 学。他很喜欢数 学。

3 Fill in the blanks with the correct words. Colour the footballs using the same colour. 提醒学生同一颜色的空位表示需写同一汉字，每种颜色只配对某一个字。学生做完题目后，仔细阅读该段落加深理解，然后可与另一个同学分别朗读一次。

学 听 衣 跑
黄色 橙色 粉色 蓝色

放 学 了，我和同 学 一起去操场踢足球。我是四号，我的运动 衣 是红色的。球来了，我 听 八号同 学 说："快 跑 、快 跑 。"

拼音输入法 Pinyin input

Circle the correct answers for inputting these characters.

a	(ai)	an	ao
1 爱	2 艾	3 矮	4 哀 ▲▼

ti	tin	tong	(ting)
1 听	2 厅	3 停	4 亭 ▲▼

ce	kei	(ke)	ker
1 课	2 颗	3 壳	4 可 ▲▼

做完题目后，提醒学生注意有的字，如"爱"，只有韵母没有声母。而大部分的字，如"听"和"课"，都有声母和韵母。

We use the 26 letters on the keyboard to input Pinyin. In the Pinyin system, there are 24 vowels including 6 simple vowels and 18 compound vowels.

a o e i u ü

ai ei ui

ao ou iu

ie üe er

an en in un ün

ang eng ing ong

老师带领学生朗读一至两遍韵母，然后让学生分小组练习。

多元学习 Connections

Cultures

告诉学生以下图片展示的是五个国家里各自比较有代表性的学校活动。让学生了解学校活动可以照顾学生不同的需要，包括品德和态度的培养、体能或技能的训练及创作力的启发等。通过参与活动，同学可以学习与人沟通和合作，同时也可以从中得到丰富的生活体验。

There are many interesting activities in schools around the world. Which one do you like? 老师可让学生在互联网上搜寻相关活动的影片并在课上分享、讨论，增加对活动的认识。

广播体操 **Radio calisthenics**

中国

Radio calisthenics are widely practised in schools. The 20-minute exercises consist of stretching, bending, jumping and other movements.

英国

橄榄球 **Rugby**

Rugby is a team game. Players can kick, carry and pass the oval ball from hand to hand.

合唱团

Singing   Austria

Choir is an organized group of singers who sometimes perform in public.

Japan

剑道 **Kendo**

Kendo is a form of fencing with two handed bamboo swords.

美国

棒球 **Baseball**

Baseball is a bat-and-ball game played between two teams who take turns batting and fielding.

Project

在做调查前，让学生尽量用中文说说学校里有哪些兴趣小组，或者有哪些兴趣小组是学校没有但学生希望可以成立的。通过学生自身的体验，拉近他们的学习距离，更投入地完成这道题目。

1 Find out which extra-curricular activities are popular in your class. Write the numbers.

你喜欢数学，还是喜欢美术？

我喜欢数学。

为什么？

因为数学作业很有趣。

还有吗？

我还喜欢……

数学

音乐

地理

电脑

篮球

跑步

参考答案：
我还喜欢篮球和跑步，因为我喜欢运动。

2 Draw a histogram to show what activities your classmates like. Tell your classmates about your findings.

提醒学生根据题一的调查结果画直方图时，首先需在纵轴上标示数值。

同学们喜欢美术小组、数学小组，还有……我喜欢……因为……的活动最有趣。……小组的人最多，有……个。

（人）

数学　音乐　地理　电脑　篮球　跑步　others

直方图 (Histogram) 是一种统计报告图，由一系列高度不等的纵向条纹或线段表示数据分布的情况。一般用横轴表示数据类型，纵轴表示分布情况。

 温习 Checkpoint

游戏方法：
学生两人一组，首先完成蓝色框里的任务，然后做相应的数学题，以此类推，直到做完红色框的相应数学题为完结。老师可提高竞争性，让全班进行比赛，最快最准完成游戏的小组为胜。

1 Play with your friend. Complete the tasks in each colour group, then finish the mathematics questions.

28  Say 'playground' in Chinese. 操场	**123** 我们一起上课。	**5**  Does he know? Answer in Chinese. 他不知道。	**16**  放学后，我回家做英语作业，还有数学作业。
+	**−**	**×**	**÷**
59  Say 'There are also many students in the hall.' in Chinese. 还有很多同学在礼堂。	**94**  这些是什么课？ Answer in Chinese. 这些是美术课和地理课。	**3** Write 'listen' in Chinese. 听	**4** Write to complete the sentence. 我们是同 学 。
=	**=**	**=**	**=**
87	29	15	4

评核方法：
学生两人一组，互相考察评价表内单词和句子的听说读写。交际沟通部分由老师朗读要求，学生再互相对话。
如果达到了某项技能要求，则用色笔将星星或小辣椒涂色。

2 Work with your friend. Colour the stars and the chillies.

Words	说	读	写
放学	☆	☆	🌶
一起	☆	☆	🌶
听	☆	☆	☆
美术	☆	☆	🌶
数学	☆	☆	🌶
上课	☆	☆	🌶
作业	☆	☆	🌶
还有	☆	☆	🌶
同学	☆	🌶	🌶
操场	☆	🌶	🌶

Words and sentences	说	读	写
礼堂	☆	🌶	🌶
地理	☆	🌶	🌶
知道	☆	🌶	🌶
还有很多同学在礼堂。	☆	🌶	🌶
这里还有美术小组和数学小组。	☆	🌶	🌶

Say the names of subjects	☆

3 What does your teacher say?

My teacher says …

评核建议：
根据学生课堂表现，分别给予"太棒了！(Excellent!)"、"不错！(Good!)"或"继续努力！(Work harder!)"的评价，再让学生圈出上方对应的表情，以记录自己的学习情况。

分享 Sharing

延伸活动：
1 学生用手遮盖英文，读中文单词，并思考单词意思；
2 学生用手遮盖中文单词，看着英文说出对应的中文单词；
3 学生三人一组，尽量运用中文单词分角色复述故事。

Words I remember

放学	fàng xué	school is over
一起	yī qǐ	together
听	tīng	to listen
美术	měi shù	art
数学	shù xué	mathematics
上课	shàng kè	to attend a class
作业	zuò yè	homework
还有	hái yǒu	also
同学	tóng xué	classmate, schoolmate
操场	cāo chǎng	playground
礼堂	lǐ táng	hall, auditorium
地理	dì lǐ	geography
知道	zhī dào	to know

Other words

大家	dà jiā	everybody
兴趣	xìng qù	interest
小组	xiǎo zǔ	group
报名	bào míng	to sign up
参加	cān jiā	to join
热闹	rè nao	lively
音乐	yīn yuè	music
游戏	yóu xì	game
更	gèng	even more
有趣	yǒu qù	interesting
这么	zhè me	so
选	xuǎn	to select
学校	xué xiào	school
吧	ba	(used at the end of a sentence to soften the tone)

Oxford University Press is a department of the University of Oxford.
It furthers the University's objective of excellence in research, scholarship,
and education by publishing worldwide. Oxford is a registered trade mark of
Oxford University Press in the UK and in certain other countries

Published in Hong Kong by
Oxford University Press (China) Limited
39th Floor, One Kowloon, 1 Wang Yuen Street, Kowloon Bay,
Hong Kong

Illustrated by Anne Lee and Wildman

Photographs for reproduction permitted by Dreamstime.com

China National Publications Import & Export (Group) Corporation is an authorized distributor of
Oxford Elementary Chinese.

Please contact content@cnpiec.com.cn or 86-10-65856782

ISBN: 978-0-19-082251-4

10 9 8 7 6 5 4 3 2

Teacher's Edition
ISBN: 978-0-19-082263-7

10 9 8 7 6 5 4 3 2